THE

NEW GOSPEL

OF

PEACE

ACCORDING TO

ST. BENJAMIN.

SINCLAIR TOUSEY,
121 NASSAU STREET, NEW YORK.
General Agent for Newsdealers and Booksellers.

Entered according to Act of Congress, in the year 1863,
By SINCLAIR TOUSEY
In the Clerk's Office of the District Court of the United States for the Southern District of New York.

THE NEW GOSPEL OF PEACE

ACCORDING TO ST. BENJAMIN.

CHAPTER I.

1 *The Mystery.* 2 *War in the Land of Unculpsalm.* 5 *Phernandiwud.* 10 *Seeketh a partner.* 17 *Searcheth the Scripture.* 19 *Findeth something to his advantage.* 24 *And walketh slantindicularly.* 25 *Is brought before the Judge.* 27 *Showeth his innocence.*

1. The mystery of the new gospel of peace.

2. In the days of Abraham, when there was war in the land of Unculpsalm, and all the people fought with weapons of iron, and with ships of iron

3. (For there came a man out of the country beyond the North Sea, a son of Tubal Cain, and joined himself unto the people of Unculpsalm, and made unto them ships of iron, with towers upon the decks thereof, and beaks upon the prows thereof, very mighty and marvellous),

4. There went out one who preached a new gospel of peace. And it was in this wise.

5. It came to pass in those days that in the country of Mannatton, in the city which is called Gotham, that is over against Jarzee, as thou goest down by the great river, the River Hutzoon, to Communipah, there was a man whose name was Phernandiwud.

6. And he was a just man, and a righteous; and he walked uprightly before the world.

7. But when he was not before the world his walk was slantindicular.

8. And he loved the people.

9. And Phernandiwud said within himself, Of a truth I love the people; but am I not one of the people; yea verily, am I not number one of the people? and shall I not therefore first love myself?

10. So Phernandiwud first loved himself, and the rest of the people after himself.

11. Now in the days when Phranclinn ruled the land (he that was captain of a thousand in the armies of Unculpsalm when they went down into Mecsichoh), Phernandiwud sought unto himself a partner, even a partner with shekels; and he found a man whose name was Marahvine.

12. And Phernandiwud said unto Marahvine: Lo there is gold in the land of Kalaphorni;

13. And the gold of that land is good.

14. Now behold thou art rich, and thy servant is poor; but thy servant is cunning in merchandise, diligent and crafty in business. Let therefore my lord furnish me of his gold and his silver, and I will buy merchandise and ships, and trade with the men of Kalaphorni and get great gain, a hundred, yea even two hundred fold, and we shall divide the spoil.

15. So they traded with the men of Kalaphorni, and got great gain, a hundred and two hundred fold. But Phernandiwud divided not the spoil; for he was not before the world.

16. So his walk was slantindicular.

17. And he communed within himself, and said: Is it not written in the Scripture (for he was a just man and a righteous, and searched the Scripture daily,

18. Saying, peradventure I shall find therein something to my advantage),

19. That a certain steward made unto himself friends of the mammon of unrighteousness, by saying to one man,

who owed his lord an hundred measures of oil, Take thy bill and sit down quickly and write fifty; and to another who owed an hundred measures of wheat, Take thy bill and sit down quickly and write fourscore?

20. And did not the lord of that steward commend him because he had done wisely; because the children of this world are wiser in their generation than the children of light?

21. And am not I, even I, Phernandiwud, a child of this world, and wise in my generation? Yea, verily. And I will take *my* bill and sit down quickly; and where Marahvine oweth me fourscore shekels, I will write an hundred; and where I owe him an hundred, I will write fifty.

22. And is it not written that we shall be as wise as serpents and as harmless as doves? Therefore will I be as wise as a serpent unto Marahvine, and as harmless as a dove unto myself.

23. Then Phernandiwud took his bill and sat down quickly, and where Marahvine owed him fourscore shekels he wrote an hundred, and where he owed Marahvine an hundred he wrote fifty.

24. So his walk was slantindicular

25. But it came to pass after many days that Marahvine discovered how Phernandiwud had searched the Scripture to his advantage. And he brought him before the judge, and would have convicted him at the mouth of two witnesses; and, moreover, the writings were against him.

26. But there was a statute in Gotham that no man should be held guilty before the law save for that which he had done within six years, but that after six years he should go free.

27. So Phernandiwud said unto the judge: Lo, what Marahvine saith that thy servant hath done was done, by his own showing, six years and three hours ago. Therefore thy servant is guiltless. I pray thee, therefore, declare thy servant guiltless, and let him go.

28. And he did so. And Phernandiwud went out from before him justified in his wisdom and his innocence.

CHAPTER II.

1 *The Pahdees.* 2 *They govern Gotham.* 5 *Phernandiwud maketh friends of the Pahdees.* 8 *Who make him Chief Ruler of the City.* 10 *And together they devour the substance of the Men of Gotham.* 14 *The Watchmen of Gotham removed from the rule of Phernandiwud.* 17 *Who gathereth together the Hittites and the Hammerites.* 18 *And conceiveth with the Mystery of the New Gospel of Peace.*

1. Now, it came to pass that in the city of Gotham were many Pahdees, like unto locusts for multitude. And they were not of the land of Unculpsalm, but came from an island beyond the great sea; a land of famine and oppression. And they knew nothing. They read not, neither did they write, and like the multitudes of Nineveh, many of them did not know their right hand from their left.

2. Therefore the men of Unculpsalm, who dwelt in Gotham, troubled themselves little to govern the city, and paid the Pahdees richly to govern it for them.

3. For the men of Gotham were great merchants and artificers, trading to the ends of the earth; diligent and cunning in their business, wise and orderly in their households; and they got great gain, and the fame of their wisdom and their diligence was spread abroad. Wherefore they said, why shall we leave our crafts and our merchandise, and our ships, and our feasts, and the gathering together of our wives and our daughters, and our men-singers and our women-singers, to give our time to ruling the city? Behold, here are the Pahdees who know nothing, who read not, neither do they write, and who know not their right hand from their left, and who have never

governed even themselves, and who will be glad to govern the city in our stead.

4. Wherefore the men of Unculpsalm who dwelt in Gotham, went the one to his craft, the other to his ships, and the other to his merchandise; and the Pahdees governed Gotham.

5. Now Phernandiwud saw that the men whom the Pahdees appointed to be officers in Gotham fed at the public crib, and waxed fat, and increased in substance. Moreover, so great and mighty was the city of Gotham that they who ruled it were powerful in the land of Unculpsalm; stretching out their hands from the North even unto the South, and from the East even unto the West; but most of all were they powerful with the men of the South.

6. And Phernandiwud said within himself, Shall I not feed at the public crib, and wax fat, and increase in substance, and become a man of power in the land of Unculpsalm?

7. So he made friends unto himself among the Pahdees, and of certain men of Unculpsalm who had joined themselves unto the Pahdees, and who called themselves Dimmichrats.

8. And he became a great man among them. And they made him chief ruler of the city. And it was of the Pahdees that he was first called Phernandiwud.

9. Now, when Phernandiwud was chief ruler of Gotham, the Pahdees, and the men of Unculpsalm which were also Dimmichrats, did what was right in their own eyes; and they worked confusion in the city, and devoured the substance of the men of Gotham. And the watchmen of the city were as clay in the hands of Phernandiwud.

10. For he said, I will have a one man power; and the one man shall be me, even me Phernandiwud; and the Pahdees, and the Dimmichrats, and the watchmen of Gotham, shall do my will; and after they have done my

will they may do what is right in their own eyes, and work confusion, and devour the people's substance.

11. And the men of Gotham were amazed and confounded; and they said one to another,

12. Behold, we are held as naught by Phernandiwud and them that are under him, and he will destroy us and our city.

13. But they could not cast him out, because of the Pahdees, and the men of Unculpsalm who also were Dimmichrats.

14. Wherefore they said, we will pray the governor and rulers of the province to take the watchmen of the city from under his hand, and put in other watchmen who shall guard the city, and the country round about the same; and he shall no longer work confusion, and devour our substance, and destroy our city.

15. Wherefore the watchmen were taken from under his rule, and there were appointed other watchmen, whose captains were not Pahdees and followers of Phernandiwud.

16. But Phernandiwud, because he loved the people, and himself first, as number one of the people, withstood the watchmen which the governor and the rulers of the province had appointed. And he gathered together his watchmen and much people of the Pahdees, and of the men of Unculpsalm which also were Dimmichrats,

17. Hittites, so-called, because they hit from the shoulder, and Hammerites, because they brake the heads of all them that set themselves up against them.

18. And the watchmen of Phernandiwud, and the Pahdees, and the Hittites and the Hammerites, fought with the watchmen appointed by the governor and chief rulers of the province, doing in this the will of Phernandiwud. And they fought many times, and they brake each the heads of the other: yet was neither vanquished.

19. And when the judges of the province saw this, they declared unto the governor, that by the great law of the

province, he could march an army upon Phernandiwud, and his watchmen, and his Pahdees, and his Hittites, and his Hammerites, and put them to the sword.

20. And when Phernandiwud read this declaration of the judges, he saw that there was an end of his rule over the watchmen, of his one man power in Gotham, and he said unto the watchmen, and to the Pahdees, and the Hittites, and the Hammerites, Get you to your houses, I have nothing more to give unto you.

21. But he charged the cost thereof unto the city.

22. And this was the first time that Phernandiwud conceived in his mind the mystery of the new gospel of peace

---

CHAPTER III.

1 *The War in the land of. Unculpsalm.* 3 *The Great Covenant.* 5 *The greatness of the land of Unculpsalm.* 7 *Provoketh the hatred of Kings and Oppressors.* 8 *The Niggahs.* 11 *And the Covenant concerning them.* 14 *The Niggahs.* 16 *There arise men of Belial.* 19 *The Tshivulree.* 22 *And what the Tshivulree did to the men of Belial.* 24 *The Dimmichrats join themselves unto the Tshivulree.* 26 *The Everlasting Niggah.* 27*Philip of Athens, a Priest of Beelzebub.* 29 *Isaiah thrusteth him out of the Tabernacle.* 31 *But the Men of Belial prevail.* 35 *And the spirit Bak Bohn possesseth their Disciples.* 39 *The Phiretahs and Prestenbruux.*

1. Now the war in the land of Unculpsalm was in this wise.

2. The people were of one blood, but the land was in many provinces. And the people of the provinces joined themselves together and cast off the yoke of a stubborn king who oppressed them beyond the great sea. And they said let us have no king, but let us choose from ourselves a man to rule over us; and let us no longer be many provinces, but one nation; only in those things which con-

cern not the nation let the people in each province do what is right in their own eyes.

3. And let it be written upon parchment and be for a covenant between us and our children, and our children's children forever—like unto a law of the Medes and Persians which altereth not.

4. And they did so. And the Great Covenant became the beginning and the end of all things unto the men of Unculpsalm.

5. And the men of Unculpsalm waxed great and mighty and rich: and the earth was filled with the fame of their power and their riches; and their ships covered the sea. And all nations feared them. But they were men of peace, and went not to war of their own accord; neither did they trouble or oppress the men of other nations; but sought each man to sit under his own vine and his own fig tree. And there were no poor men and few that did evil born in that land: except thou go southward of the border of Masunandicsun.

6. And this was noised abroad; and it came to pass that the poor and the down-trodden, and the oppressed of other lands left the lands in which they were born, and went and dwelt in the land of Unculpsalm, and prospered therein, and no man molested them. And they loved that land.

7. Wherefore, the kings and the oppressors of other lands, and they that devoured the substance of the people, hated the men of Unculpsalm. Yet, although they were men of peace, they made not war upon them; for they were many and mighty. Moreover they were rich and bought merchandise of other nations, and sent them corn and gold.

8. Now there were in the land of Unculpsalm Ethiopians, which the men of Unculpsalm called Niggahs. And their skins were black, and for hair they had wool, and their shins bent out forward and their heels thrust out backward; and their ill savor went up

9. Wherefore the forefathers of the men of Unculpsalm had made slaves of the Niggahs, and bought them and sold them like cattle.

10. But so it was that when the people of the land of Unculpsalm made themselves into one nation, the men of the North said, We will no longer buy and sell the Niggahs, but will set them free; neither shall more be brought from Ethiopia for slaves unto this land.

11. And the men of the South answered and said, We will buy and sell our Niggahs; and moreover we will beat them with stripes, and they shall be our hewers of wood and drawers of water forever; and when our Niggahs flee into your provinces ye shall give them to us, every man his Niggah; and after a time there shall no more be brought from Ethiopia, as ye say. And this shall be a part of the great covenant.

12. And it was a covenant between the men of the North and the men of the South.

13. And it came to pass that thereafter the men of the South and the Dimmichrats of the North, and the Pahdees gave themselves night and day to the preservation of this covenant about the Niggahs.

14. And the Niggahs increased and multiplied till they darkened all the land of the South. And the men of Unculpsalm who dwelt in the South took their women for concubines and went in unto them, and begat of them sons and daughters. And they bought and sold their sons and daughters, even the fruit of their loins; and beat them with stripes, and made them hewers of wood and drawers of water.

15. For they said, Are not these Niggahs our Niggahs? Yea, even more than the other Niggahs? For the other Niggahs we bought, or our fathers, with money; but these, are they not flesh of our flesh, and blood of our blood, and bone of our bone; and shall we not do what we will with our own?

16. But there arose men in the northern provinces of the land of Unculpsalm and in the countries beyond the great sea, iniquitous men, saying, Man's blood cannot be bought with money; foolish men saying, Though the Niggah's skin be black and his hair woolly, and his shins like unto cucumbers, and his heels thursting out backward, and though he have an ill savor not to be endured by those who get not children of Niggah women, is yet a man; men of Belial which said, All things whatsoever ye would that men should do to you, do ye even so to them; for this is the law and the prophets.

17. And the slaves were for a reproach throughout all the world unto the men of the South, and even to the whole land of Unculpsalm. But by reason of the great covenant and the laws of the provinces, the men of the North had naught to do in this matter.

18. But the men of the South which had Niggahs (for there were multitudes which had no Niggahs, and they were poor and oppressed) heeded it not; for they were a stiff-necked generation. And they said, we will not let our Niggahs go free; for they are our chattels, even as our horses and our sheep, our swine and our oxen; and we will beat them, and slay them, and sell them, and beget children of them, and no man shall gainsay us. We stand by the Great Covenant.

19. Moreover we are Tshivulree.

20. Now to be of the Tshivulree was the chief boast among the men of the South, because it had been a great name upon the earth. For of olden time he who was of the Tshivulree was bound by an oath to defend the weak and succor the oppressed, yea, even though he gave his life for them. But among the men of the South he only was of the Tshivulree who ate his bread in the sweat of another's face, who robbed the laborer of his hire, who oppressed the weak, and set his foot upon the neck of the lowly, and who sold from the mother the fruit of her

womb and the nursling of her bosom. Wherefore the name of Tshivulree stank in the nostrils of all the nations.

21. For they were in the darkness of a false dispensation, and had not yet learned the mystery of the new gospel of peace.

22. And when the Tshivulree found within their borders those men of the North, iniquitous men which said that man's blood cannot be bought, and men of Belial which said, Do ye unto all men as ye would have all men do unto you, they seized upon them and beat them with many stripes, and hanged them upon trees, and roasted them with fire, and poured hot pitch upon them, and rode them upon sharp beams, very grievous to bestride, and persecuted them even as it was fitting such pestilent fellows should be persecuted.

23. And they said unto the men of the North, cease ye now to send among us these men of Belial preaching iniquity, cease also to listen unto them yourselves, and respect the Great Covenant, or we will destroy this nation.

24. Then the men of Unculpsalm which called themselves Dimmichrats, and the Pahdees, seeing that the Tshivulree of the South had only one thought, and that was for the Niggah, said, We will join ourselves unto the Tshivulree, and we will have but one thought with them, even the Niggah; and we shall rule the land of Unculpsalm, and we shall divide the spoil.

25. And they joined themselves unto the Tshivulree; and the Tshivulree of the South, and the men of the North, which called themselves Dimmichrats, and the Pahdees ruled the land of Unculpsalm for many years; and they divided the spoil. And they had but one thought, even for the Niggah.

26. Wherefore he was called the everlasting Niggah.

27. Now, about these days came Philip, from the new Athens, a priest of Beelzebub, and he taught in the Tabernacle at Gotham.

28. And Philip had many words, but only one thought; and that, like the thought of the men of the South, was for the Niggah. But he respected not the Great Covenant. And he said unto the people ye ought to set the Niggah free.

29. And it came to pass that when he was teaching in the Tabernacle one Isaiah entered (not the prophet, but he who was captain of a band of the Hammerites) and protested unto him that he should no more teach such pestilent doctrine. And having his band of Hammerites with him, he knocked Philip down, and thrust him from the pulpit wherein he was speaking, and drave him out of the Tabernacle.

30. Now this was the first ministration of the new gospel of peace. But as yet it was not preached; for it had no apostle.

31. But in process of time the ministers of Belial turned the hearts of many men, even of them which called themselves Dimmichrats to iniquity; and they all began to say that the strength of the great nation of Unculpsalm should not be used to oppress the Niggah; declaring in the wickedness of their imaginations and the hardness of their hearts, that whatsoever the people of Unculpsalm would that others should do to them even so they should do to others, even unto Niggahs.

32. But they had respect unto the Great Covenant, and sought not to set the Niggahs free; and they returned unto the men of the South the Niggahs that fled from their provinces, according to the Great Covenant.

33. Moreover the men of the North made soft answers unto the men of the South, and strove to turn away their wrath, and to live with them as brethren. For though they feared them not, neither hated them, they did fear that they would destroy the nation.

34. And the Tshivulree of the South saw that the men of the North feared their threats; and they waxed bolder

and said, We will not only keep our Niggahs in our own provinces, but we will take them into all the country of Unculpsalm, which is not yet divided into provinces. And they went roaring up and down the land.

35. But in process of time it came to pass that the spirit of their forefathers appeared among the men of the North, even the great spirit Bak Bohn; and he stiffened up the people mightily.

36. So that they said unto the men of the South, Hear us, our brethren! We would live with you in peace, and love you, and respect the Great Covenant. And the Niggahs in your provinces ye shall keep, and slay, and sell, they and the children which ye beget of them, into slavery, for bond men and bond women for ever. Yours be the sin before the Lord, not ours; for it is your doing, and we are not answerable for it. And your Niggahs that flee from your provinces they shall be returned unto you, according to the Great Covenant. Only take care lest peradventure ye make captives the Niggahs of our provinces which we have made free men. Ye shall in no wise take a Niggah of them.

37. Thus shall it be with your Niggahs and in your provinces, and yours shall be the blame forever. But out of your provinces, into the common land of Unculpsalm, ye shall not carry your Niggahs except they be made thereby free. For that land is common, and your laws and the statutes of your provinces, by which alone ye make bondmen, run not in that land. And for all that is done in that land we must bear the blame with you. For that land is common; and we share whatever is done therein; and the power of this nation and the might of its banner shall no longer be used to oppress the lowly and to fasten the chain upon the captive. Keep ye then your bondmen within your own provinces.

38. Then the Tshivulree of the South waxed wroth, and foamed in their anger, and the air of the land was filled

with their cursings and their revilings. And certain of them which were men of blood, and which were possessed of devils, and had difficulties, and slew each other with knives and shooting irons, did nothing all their time but rave through the land about the Niggah.

39. Now these men were the fore-runners of him that preached the new gospel of peace, and prepared the way before him. Wherefore they were called Phiretahs.

40. And it came to pass that one of the Phiretahs, whose name was Prestenbruux, was wroth with Charles, who was surnamed the Summoner, who was one of the chief law-givers of the land of Unculpsalm, and also one of the men of Belial, who taught iniquity, saying, Whatsoever ye would that men should do to you do ye even so to them, even unto Niggahs.

For Charles the Summoner had declared that it was not lawful for the men of the South to take their Niggahs out of their own provinces. And thus it was that Prestenbruux was offended in him.

41. Wherefore Prestenbruux took unto himself other Phiretahs, and he sought Charles the Summoner, and found him alone at a table, writing in the great hall of Unculpsalm. And he came upon him unawares, and he smote him and beat him to the ground, so that he was nigh unto death.

42. And this was the second ministration of the new gospel of peace. But even now it was not preached, for it had yet no apostle.

43. And after these things, James, whose surname being interpreted meaneth Facing-both-ways, ruled in the land of Unculpsalm.

CHAPTER IV.

1 *The choice of Abraham the Honest.* 10 *The Phiretahs rebel against him.* 14 *Compromise.* 17 *The Phiretahs will have no more Compromise.* 18 *Ken Edee and Robert of Joarji.* 23 *Phernandiwud compromiseth unto Robert.* 24 *The men of the North wax wroth.*

1. Now the time drew nigh when James should cease to rule in the land of Unculpsalm.

2. And the men of the North, save the Dimmichrats, among whom were the Pahdees, strove to have Abraham, who was surnamed the honest, made ruler in the place of James Facing-both-ways.

3. But the Phiretahs of the South said, Let us choose, and let the voices be numbered, and if our man be chosen, it is well, but if Abraham, we will destroy the nation.

4. But the men of the North believed them not, because of the Great Covenant, and because they trusted them to be of good faith in this matter. For among the men of the North, even those who lived by casting lots for gold, stood by the lot when it was cast. And the men of the North believed not that men of their own blood, whose sons were married unto their daughters, and whose daughters unto their sons, would faithlessly do this thing which they threatened.

5. But the men of the North knew not how the Niggah had driven out all other thoughts from the hearts of the men of the South, even so that they would violate the Great Covenant, and set at naught the election according thereunto if it went against them.

6. And there were throughout the provinces of the land of Unculpsalm at the North great multitudes, Dimmichrats, of whom were the Pahdees, who were friends of the Phiretahs of the South, and wished them well, and labored with them; for they said, It is by the alliance of the men

of the South, and by reason of the everlasting Niggah, that we rule the land.

7. But they deceived themselves; for it was the Phiretahs which ruled the land, using the Dimmichrats, and by the one thought of the everlasting Niggah.

8. Yet it came to pass that when the voices of the people were numbered, according to the Great Covenant, Abraham was chosen.

9. Then the Phiretahs of the South began to do as they had threatened; and they gathered together in their provinces, and said, Our provinces shall no longer be a part of the land of Unculpsalm, for we will not have this man Abraham to rule over us.

10. Yet were there men of the South, a great multitude, among whom was Stephen, of Joarji, who said, Not so. Why will ye do this great evil and destroy the nation? It is right for us to respect the Great Covenant. If the man who had our voices had been chosen, the men of the North would have received him, and obeyed him as the chief ruler in the land of Unculpsalm; and it is meet and right that we should do likewise, even according to the Great Covenant. Moreover, we have suffered no wrong at the hands of the new rulers; and the old were men of our own choosing. Will ye make this land like unto Mecsicho?

11. But the Phiretahs would not hearken unto these men, and went on their way, and beat some of them, and hanged others, and threatened noisily, and gathering unto them all the people of the baser sort, and inflaming them with hate and strong drink, they set up a rule of terror throughout their provinces. For the Phiretahs were men of blood. So the Phiretahs prevailed over the men who would have respected the Great Covenant.

12. And the men of the North, both they who had given their voices for Abraham and they who had given their voices with the men of the South against him, were

amazed and stood astounded. And they said among themselves, This is vain boasting and vaunting, such as we have seen aforetime, done for the sake of more compromise.

13. (Now in the land of Unculpsalm, when a man humbled himself before another which threatened him, he was said to compromise.)

14. And the Dimmichrats, save those who had hearkened unto the ministers of Belial, said, Let us compromise ourselves again unto our Southern brethren, and it shall be well with us.

15. For they said among themselves, If the men of the South go, they and their provinces, there will be no more everlasting Niggah; and we shall cease to rule the land. And if they go not, behold then they will remember that we have compromised unto them, and they will again be gracious unto their servants, and will admit us unto a share in the government, and we shall rule the land as aforetime.

16. But the Phiretahs were wise in their generation, and they saw that the Dimmichrats were of no more use unto them, and that because the men of Belial had prevailed against the Dimmichrats, their power was gone in in their provinces; and so as they could no more use the Dimmichrats, they would not listen to them, and spurned their compromising, and spat upon it, and went on to destroy the nation, and prepared to make war against Abraham if he should begin to rule over them.

17. Now in those days there was a man in Gotham named Ken Edee, who was chief captain of the watchmen of the city and the region round about; and in Joarji was a man named Robert, who dwelt among the tombs, and who was possessed of an evil spirit whose name was Blustah. And Robert was a Phiretah.

18. And Ken Edee, chief captain of the watch in Gotham, found arms going from Gotham to the Phiretahs in Joarji, and he seized them. For he said, Lest they be

used to destroy the nation, and against the Great Covenant, which is the supreme law in the land of Unculpsalm, to which first belongeth my obedience.

19. Then Robert, who dwelt among the tombs, being seized upon by his demon Blustah, sent a threatening message unto Phernandiwud.

20. (For at this time Phernandiwud was chief ruler in the city of Gotham.)

21. Saying, Wherefore keep ye the arms of the Phiretahs? Give them unto us that we may make war against you, or it shall be worse for you.

22. Then Phernandiwud, because he hated the chief of the watchmen of Gotham, and because he hoped for the good success of the Phiretahs, compromised himself unto Robert, and crawled on his belly before him in the dust, and said, Is thy servant a man that he should do this thing? Thy servant kept no arms, neither would he do so. Let them who have the evil spirit Bak Bohn do thus unto my lords the Phiretahs. Behold, thy servant is no man, but a Phlunkee.

23. (Now the Phlunkees were men who had never had the spirit Bak Bohn, or who had had it cast out of them, because when they would have prostrated themselves and humbled themselves in the dust and compromised to their profit, the spirit rent them sore. So they had each of them his Bak Bohn cast out of him.)

24. And the Phiretahs went on their way without hindrance. For James, by facing both ways, faced neither; and both of the men of the South and the men of the North he was not regarded. And the nation spued him out of its mouth.

25. And Abraham ruled the land. But the Phiretahs withstood him, and made war upon him, and drove his captains out of the strongholds which were in their provinces, and humbled the banner of Unculpsalm.

26. Then all the men of the North, even the Dimmi-

chrats, of whom were the Pahdees, were exceeding wroth; and they rose up against the Phiretahs of the South, and marched against them to drive them out of the strong places which they had seized, and to plant thereon again the banner of Unculpsalm.

27. For they all had exceeding reverence for the Great Covenant, and they were filled with pride of their nation, its might, and its wealth, and its vastness, and chiefly that its people were more free than any other people, and that its tillers of the soil and its wayfaring men could read and understand, and that there each man sat under his own vine and under his own fig tree with none to molest him or make him afraid. And they worshipped the banner of Unculpsalm, and its folds were unto them as the wings of a protecting angel.

28. Moreover, the Dimmichrats said, We have striven for our brethren of the South against the men of Belial, who teach that it is wrong to oppress the Niggah by the power of Unculpsalm, and now they can no longer use us they cast us off. Behold, we will fight against them, lest, also, they make good their threats, and sever their provinces from our provinces, and there be no more everlasting Niggah, and our occupation be departed forever.

29. And thus it came to pass that there was war in the land of Unculpsalm.

CHAPTER V.

1 *The Men of Gotham assemble.* 2 *Having each a Bak Bohn.* 3 *And Phernandiwud getteth a Bak Bohn.* 5 *And speaketh to the People.* 8 *Benjamin the Scribe goeth not to the Assembly, but remaineth at home, mourning.* 13 *His policy and his prosperity.* 18 *The War continueth for two years.* 19 *And why.* 26 *The Rulers of Jonbool help the Phiretahs.*

1. Now, when the news came that the Phiretahs of the South with five thousand men, even a great multitude, had

driven one of the captains of Unculpsalm with a band of ninety out of his stronghold, and when a proclamation of Abraham was spread abroad, calling on the men of Unculpsalm for the defence of their nation, and the retaking of its strongholds, and the setting up of its banner which had been cast down, the men of Gotham gathered themselves together in an open place before the world. And Phernandiwud came also among them.

2. And each man that day out of whom had been cast the spirit Bak Bohn, took to himself another worse than the first. And it seemed that day that in all Gotham there was not one Phlunkee.

3. And Phernandiwud saw this. So he also straightway took to himself a Bak Bohn.

4. For he said, Lest they also declare that I shall no longer be chief ruler of the city.

5. And many men of Gotham spake unto the people. Phernandiwud also lifted up his voice and said, Hear O men of Unculpsalm! give ear, O men of Gotham! The rulers of this land of Unculpsalm chosen according to the Great Covenant have been defied. The Great Covenant itself hath been set at naught. The banner of Unculpsalm hath been cast down. The men of the South begin to make good their threats that they would destroy this nation.

6. But I say unto you, in the words of the great ruler Jah Xunn, whom to our sorrow we have gathered to his fathers, This nation must and shall be preserved, peaceably if we can, forcibly if we must. And let us have a strong rule and a splendid despotism, that we may do this thing as becometh a great nation. For I have said always aforetime, as ye can bear me witness, Let us strengthen the hands of the chief rulers, being myself chief ruler of this city. Hear therefore my pledge unto you this day, I throw myself wholly into this strife, with all my power and with all my might.

7. Now there were men who noted that Phernandiwud pledged himself with all his power and with all his might, but not with all his soul. And they said, It is because he hath sold his soul unto the mighty spirit Sathanas, that he should help him. And others said, Not so; for he had no soul to sell. But these were scoffers and men of Belial.

8. But Benjamin, the brother of Phernandiwud, even Benjamin the scribe, came not unto the congregation of the people, but remained at home in his house, exceeding wroth and very sorrowful. For he said, Behold this people is given over to the spirit Bak Bohn, and into the hands of the men of Belial, who teach that the power of Unculpsalm, and the might of the banner of Unculpsalm, may not be used to oppress the Niggah. And this people will no more compromise itself before the men of the South; and there will be no more Phlunkees, and the everlasting Niggah shall cease from off the land. And he wept him sore; and cried out aloud, The sceptre hath departed from the Dimmichrats, and the glory from the tents of Tamunee!

9. And he wrote against the people of the North; and sought to exorcise the mighty spirit Bak Bohn, and to cast it out of them. But he could not.

10. Now Benjamin the scribe was also a just man, and a righteous, and walked uprightly before the law.

11. For the law said, Thou shalt not live by casting lots for gold. For he who liveth by casting lots for gold deceiveth the foolish man to his hurt, and defraudeth the widow and the fatherless. It is an abomination. And he that liveth by casting lots for gold shall be guilty and shall be cast into prison.

12. Wherefore Benjamin being a just man and a righteous, said, I will not live by casting lots for gold. Far be it from me to do this thing which is unlawful, and which will get me into prison. But I will sell policies; and this shall be the craft by which I will live.

13. For what saith the prophet Daniel (not Sickles)? "And through his policy also shall he cause craft to prosper in his hand; and he shall magnify himself in his heart."

14. For Benjamin also searched the Scripture, saying: Peradventure I may find therein something to my advantage.

15. Wherefore Benjamin the scribe, through his policies caused craft to prosper in his hand, and magnified himself in his heart.

16. And he said within himself, I will be a lawgiver in the land of Unculpsalm, even for the men of Gotham. Wherefore, he also made unto himself friends among the Pahdees; and he became a lawgiver in the land.

17. But the men of Gotham cast out Phernandiwud from his office of chief ruler of the city; because they remembered that he had compromised upon his belly to Robert who dwelt among the tombs, and had eaten dirt before him. Also that he had said, Let us take our city out of the nation. So they put no trust in him.

18. Now so it was that after the space of nearly two years the war which was in the land of Unculpsalm came not to an end.

19. For the men of the North and the men of the South were of one blood; and both were valiant. And the men of the North were more in number than the men of the South. But the men of the South multiplied themselves because of their Niggahs. For their Niggahs went not to war, but stayed at home to till the soil. Moreover, they were fighting upon their own ground; and much of their land was mire and marshes, desert land and wilderness, through which the armies of Unculpsalm wandered vainly, and where they stuck fast. And the men of the South cast up mounds upon their roads, and before their cities, and made strong their high places with towers. And their land was filled with strong places, and with men of war and engines of war, such as the men of the North looked not to see in that land.

20. For the men of the South were astonished when the men of the North marched against them; because the men of the North had so often compromised themselves unto them, that they thought they were all Phlunkees, and that the spirit Bak Bohn had been utterly cast out of them. And without that spirit men cannot fight.

21. Wherefore, the men of the South which had Niggahs, even the Tshivulree and the Phiretahs, seeing that their case was desperate, forced all the men of their country into their armies, and took the men which had respect unto the government of Unculpsalm, according to the Great Covenant, and loved the banner of Unculpsalm, and would not fight against it, and they cast them into pits and into dungeons, and scourged them, and hanged them upon trees, after their manner. And being men of blood, and seeing that their case was desperate, they made it a terror to live in their country except unto them that professed to desire the destruction of the nation. So all men professed to desire it, or held their peace.

22. But in the land of the men of the North no man was molested. And men of the South dwelt there, and were spies and helpers unto their brethren. And men of the North, men of peace, which also were Phlunkees, helped their masters the Tshivulree and the Phiretahs.

23. And the men of the South had among them great captains; men of might and wisdom in battle. And they chose to be ruler over them Jeph, surnamed the Repudiator.

24. (Now among the men of Unculpsalm when a man would neither pay the debt that he owed, nor acknowledge it and ask it to be forgiven him, he was called a repudiator.)

25. And Jeph had been captain over a thousand in the armies of Unculpsalm when they went into Mecsicho, and had also been one of the great Council: and he was a bold man, and a crafty, one who knew neither fear nor scruple.

26. Moreover, the men of the South were helped might-

ily from beyond the sea, even by the men of the kingdom of Jonbool, from which their land was wrested by the forefathers of the men of Unculpsalm.

27. Yet the men of Unculpsalm would have loved the men of that nation, even as a son loveth his mother which bore him. But the nobles and the rich men of Jonbool scorned the men of Unculpsalm, and would none of their affection, and made light of their honor.

28. For the men of Unculpsalm had forgiven the men of Jonbool their oppression and their scorn, and had shown their Prince great honor; but the men who governed that nation had not forgiven the men of Unculpsalm their victory. And the prosperity and the glory of that land was an offence unto them. And certain of their scribes, which also were Phlunkees, wrote scornfully against the land of Unculpsalm, and bore false witness against it from generation to generation, and got thereby gold and honor in the land of Jonbool.

29. Wherefore, when the Tshivulree and the Phiretahs lifted up the standard of revolt, the rulers of the land of Jonbool said one to another,

30. Lo, the time for which we have waited without hope draweth nigh; and the land of Unculpsalm may be divided, and the nation destroyed, and the pride of the people cast down. And the might of their power shall be broken, and the glory of that land shall no longer be an offence unto us; and we shall be avenged without peril and without cost.

31. Likewise, also, said the nobles and the great men of other lands, where the few devoured the substance of the many.

32. So the rulers of the land of Jonbool made proclamation to all the earth, that in that war they would regard the men of the South which had revolted even as they regarded the rulers of the land chosen according to the Great Covenant. For they said, Thus shall we encourage

them, and give aid to them; and it shall cost us nothing: and after this they will be more ashamed to submit themselves unto the law which they have broken, and to the rulers which they have defied.

33. And the nobles and the merchants of that land, which aforetime had cursed and reviled the Tshivulree and the Phiretahs, and had imputed the deeds which were theirs only unto all the men of Unculpsalm, said Amen.

34. And the merchants of Jonbool sold the Phiretahs merchandise, and the armorers made them arms, and the ship-men builded them ships, swift and mighty, wherewith to destroy the ships of the men of the North. For they said thus shall we be avenged, and turn, also, every man, an honest penny. State-craft and business shall prosper together, and profit shall go hand in hand with pleasure.

35. And thus was the rebellion strengthened in the land of Unculpsalm; so that although the armies of Unculpsalm drove the men of the South out of much country where they had set up their banners, and captured their chief cities, and held all that they had taken, yet after two years were not their armies scattered or destroyed, or their ships which the men of Jonbool had builded for them, driven from the sea.

CHAPTER VI.

1 *Abraham and his Counsellors not wise in their generation,* 6 *Which is well pleasing to certain Dimmichrats.* 10 *Who seek to work confusion.* 12 *And to compromise themselves unto the Phiretahs.* 13 *And do compromise themselves unto the Ambassador of Jonbool.* 16 *Who is crafty and turneth neither to the right nor to the wrong.* 17 *The wrath of the men of the North.* 21 *The sect of Peace Men.* 25 *The House of Hiram the Publican.* 26 *A Woman of the Phiretahs.* 28 *Samuel*

seeketh her and ministereth unto her. 30 Abraham ministereth occasion unto the Peace men. They have a martyr.

1. Now Abraham was honest; but he was not wise in his generation.

2. Likewise also of the chief counsellors that he appointed that one that was counsellor for the war wrought only mischief and confusion; even so that Abraham, who was long-suffering and slow to anger, would sometimes put down his foot in wrath.

3. Now Abraham's foot was heavy, but his head was light, and his knees were feeble. So his foot came down in the wrong place or at the wrong time, or else it continued not down until the end was accomplished.

4. Wherefore he prevailed not. And he was called Abraham the well meaning. And men pitied him.

5. And Abraham and his counsellors should have ruled with a firm hand and a mighty arm, and have bound the land together with bands of steel; and have smitten down the strong and set at naught the proud, and been gracious unto the feeble. But they wavered, and shrank from the voice of threatening, both in their own land and in the land of Jonbool.

6. And this was well pleasing unto certain men of the Dimmichrats. For they said in their hearts, If this nation can be saved by the rule of the Dimmichrats of our faction, let it be saved; but if not, let it perish, and let us rule in our own provinces.

7. But they said not this openly; for they feared the people.

8. For in all this time the hearts of the men of the North failed not, neither did they alter in their wicked purpose to preserve their nation from destruction.

9. And of the Dimmichrats it was only they who were faithful to their masters the Tshivulree and the Phiretahs, and who were meek and lowly, and who sought to com-

promise unto them, and crawl on their bellies before them, which was well fitting for them to do, and to say unto them, What would our masters have? and what shall their servants do that they may be gracious unto their servants, and allow them a little share in the ruling of this land?—it was these only among the Dimmichrats who were well pleased because Abraham and his counsellors prevailed not.

10. And these men held not up the hands of Abraham their ruler, but sought occasion to prevent his purposes and to bring his counsels to confusion, and his doings to naught.

11. And when Abraham's foot came down in the wrong place, or continued not down until the end was accomplished, and men's hearts were sick with disappointment, they sought to turn them in favor of Jeph the Repudiator and his counsellors.

12. And they said, Let us not have war with our masters the Tshivulree and the Phiretahs; but let us compromise unto them, and crawl on our bellies before them, even as we did aforetime; for it is meet and right and a pleasant thing to be humble.

13. And they sent messengers unto the Tshivulree and the Phiretahs, saying these things; and their scribes wrote them in books by night and sent them out unto the people by day. But the Tshivulree and the Phiretahs spurned them; for now that they could no more use them, they looked at them with loathing.

14. Likewise also some of them went privily to the ambassador of the land of Jonbool, even that land which sought the destruction of the nation of Unculpsalm.

15. And they said unto him, Let us take counsel together that we may bring about this great end, the ceasing of the war without the putting down of the rebellion.

16. But he was crafty and answered them nothing. And he wrote letters unto the rulers of his land, saying, I

will watch faithfully, and I will turn aside neither to the right nor to the wrong, going which way it may be needful, if it leadeth to our profit. So shall I show myself worthy to be a ruler in the land of Jonbool.

17. Now when this letter was noised abroad in the land of Unculpsalm, the men of the north were incensed, and the fire of their anger was hot against the Dimmichrats that called themselves Peace men. For upon this matter the men of Belial, and the Dimmichrats which were not Peace men, and the Pahdees were of one mind.

18. And they said, Who is it that hath dared thus to humble this nation? Let him come out before us. And no man answered.

19. For they which had done it saw that they could not stand before the people and live. Yet still they said in their hearts, If this nation can be saved by the rule of the Dimmichrats of our faction, let it be saved; but if not, let it perish, and let us rule in our own provinces. For now they had but one thought; not how the rebellious Tshivulree and Phiretahs might be subdued and compelled again to their obedience, but how they might again rule the land and divide the spoil, and have again thier everlasting Niggah.

20. Wherefore they cried aloud for war, but labored in secret to bring the war to naught, and to turn the minds of the people to peace, that they might compromise unto the Phiretahs as they did aforetime. And they watched for their occasion.

21. Now the chiefs of this sect in Gotham were these:

22. Phernandiwud, who had been chief ruler of the city, and Benjamin his brother; James the scribe, which knew nothing, and Erastus his brother; Samuel, who was rich in butter; Hiram the publican, who was also a sinner, and Elijah, who smelled the battle afar in the tents of Tamnee; Cyrus (not he that was taught to ride, to shoot the bow, and to speak the truth, yet did this Cyrus shoot

with a longer bow than the other); Primus the scribe, whose beard was like Aaron's, and who dwelt among the merchants; Samuel, who made the lightnings of heaven his messengers; Ker Tiss, who wrote concerning the Great Covenant; and one who dwelt in the elbows of the Mincio, and destroyed the hearts of women; Isaiah, who was a captain of the Hammerites; Samuel whose surname was Brinnzmaid, and whose fathers ate hasty-pudding; and Augustus the money-changer, who aforetime was called Schomberg.

23. Now the others were Gentiles, but Augustus was of the circumcision.

24. And all these men served diligently their master, who was Jeph the Repudiator. And many of them were Scribes, but all of them were Pharisees; for they held to the letter of the law, but knew not its spirit. And they taught, like them of old, concerning the Sabbath, that the nation was made for the Great Covenant, and not the Great Covenant for the nation.

25. And the inn of Hiram, which before the war began in the land of Unculpsalm had been filled with Tshivulree and Phiretahs, and with Phlunkees compromising themselves unto their masters the Phiretahs, and crawling upon their bellies before them, became now the chief place of resort for them that still served the Tshivulree and labored to prosper the rebellion. There they gathered themselves together and plotted in secret how they might ensnare the rulers of Unculpsalm, and rejoiced openly when the banner of the Phiretahs prevailed against the banner of Unculpsalm. So did the inn of Hiram become the synagogue of rebellion.

26. And there came a woman of the Phiretahs into Gotham. And she was married; yet was her husband not with her. And she was comely and fair to look upon.

27. And it was told unto the rulers of Unculpsalm, Behold, this woman of the Phiretahs cometh to spy out the

nakedness of the land. Wherefore the rulers sent a message unto Ken Edee, chief of the watchmen of Gotham, that he should take her and put her in ward. And he did so.

28. Now when Samuel, whose surname was Brinnzmaid, heard that Ken Edee had taken a woman of the Phiretahs and put her in ward, he went to her; and when he saw that her husband was not with her, and that she was comely and fair to look upon, and that she had come to spy out the nakedness of the land, he succored her and ministered unto her. And he caused Ken Edee to take her out of ward; and when he had kept her in Gotham for awhile, that she might be comforted and see the nakedness of the land, he sent her back into the land of Tshivulree.

29. So all these men, and many others which followed them, did nothing else night and day but strive to get the land again into the hands of their faction that they might serve their master Jeph the Repudiator, and compromise unto him, and preserve their everlasting Niggah.

30. Now while they were waiting their occasion, Abraham himself ministered it unto them. For one of the captains in the army of Unculpsalm, took Clement, a lawgiver, because he had said that Abraham was a usurper and a tyrant, in that he resisted Jeph the Repudiator, and had sought to diminish the armies of Unculpsalm, and cast him into prison; and to a scribe which did likewise, the captain sent armed men that stood over him with drawn swords, saying, Ye shall no longer thus stir up the people to sedition.

31. And immediately the chief men of the Dimmichrats throughout the land raised a great uproar, for they said, Now cometh our opportunity.

32. For there was a law in the land of Unculpsalm that every man might speak and write freely all the promptings of his heart, so that he slandered not his neighbor, and that no man should be cast into prison save by a judge,

when he had been condemned by twelve good men of his province. And the people of the land of Unculpsalm prized this law above all their other laws; and it was a part of the Great Covenant and of the Great Charter of the liberties of that people.

33. But it was written in the Great Covenant that in times of sedition, privy conspiracy, and rebellion, this law should cease and be of no effect; for the safety of the nation.

34. Now the leaders of the Dimmichrats, who were wise in their generation, and who sought first to get power into their own hands, and afterwards the salvation of the nation, said among themselves, Lo, Abraham has given us a martyr; and it is better than if he had given the armies of Unculpsalm a victory. Now, therefore, let us bewail the woes of Clement and the violence to the Great Covenant and the ancient Charter; and we will declare that it is to preserve this nation from destruction, and we shall regain the hearts of this people.

35. And they did so. And the people forgat the peril of the land, and how it was in more danger from traitors that were within than from foes that were without; and they forgat also the provision of the Great Covenant against such perils; and there was a great commotion.

36. And Abraham said, Let not Clement be kept in prison; but let him be sent among the Phiretahs; for they are his friends, and he is our enemy; and let the scribe continue his writing. And it was done. So Clement became a martyr; and the scribe hardened his heart and was tenfold more the servant of the Phiretahs than before. For he said, Abraham feareth the Dimmichrats, and even the men of Belial fear them also, and the spirit Bak Bohn is again cast out of them.

CHAPTER VII.

1 *Phernandiwud summoneth his disciples to hear the New Gospel of Peace at the Hall of Peter the Barrelmaker.* 8 *Who came not to the Assembly.* 9 *And why.* 13 *Who came.* 17 *Phernandiwud proclaimeth the New Gospel of Peace.* 20 *The Hittites and Hammerites are well pleased.* 22 *But have groanings about the freedom of the Niggah.* 25 *Phernandiwud showeth that there is no right but Peace and Everlasting Niggah.* 26 *And Free Speech.* 32 *Meekness of Phernandiwud.* 33 *And of the Hittites and the Hammerites.* 38 *Isaiah telleth of a ministration of Peace.* 45 *The New Gospel of Peace spreadeth beyond the border of Masunandicsun.*

1. Now Phernandiwud saw that his time was come.

2. And he said unto his familiars and to them which did his bidding, (for he had a great following in Gotham), Behold, the spirit of peace hath descended upon me; and I go forth to declare the mystery of a new gospel of peace, a gospel of great gain, unto me first, and afterward unto the Dimmichrats. And I shall reward them who are faithful unto me.

3. Go now therefore and summon the Dimmichrats who serve Jeph the Repudiator and the Phiretahs in Gotham.

4. James the scribe and Erastus his brother, who know nothing, and my brother Benjamin, who knoweth some things; Samuel, who is rich in butter, Hiram, the publican; Elijah, who smelleth the battle afar off; Cyrus, who shooteth with a longer bow than the first Cyrus; Primus, who dwelleth among the merchants; Ker Tiss, of the great Covenant; Isaiah, captain of the Hammerites; Samuel, who sendeth the lightning on his errand, and the other Samuel, whose surname is Brinnzmaid; and Augustus, the money-changer.

5. And say unto them, Gather yourselves together, ye and your following, every man of you in the hall of Peter

who is called the Barrel-maker, and in the open space round about, that ye may hear from my lips the new gospel of peace.

6. (Now this Peter made the substance whereby one thing sticketh unto another thing. Wherefore he was for union; and he called the hall which he had builded, the Union; (for he said, Thus shall I stick this nation together,) but the people called it after his own name. And he was rich and he offended no man. Now in the land of Unculpsalm, whosoever was rich and offended no man, became one of the chief men of his place, and of his country. Moreover, Peter gave of his substance unto the people. And this was he who, at a feast given unto the Prince of the land of Jonbool, clapped the Prince upon the shoulder and said unto him, My lord the Prince shall dance next with my daughter. For he was a gracious man and a courteous, and he knew that his daughter was comely.)

7. And Phernandiwud looked for the assembling of the men which he had summoned, they and their following, at the hall of Peter the Barrel-maker, and the space round about.

8. But these men came not: James the scribe, and Erastus his brother; Samuel, whose sirname is Brinnzmaid and the other Samuel; Benjamin the brother of Phernandiwudd, and Elijah of Tamunee; Hiram the publican, and Cyrus, Primus, and Augustus the money-changer, and their following.

9. For they said within themselves, This gospel of peace will be an offence unto the people, who are preverse in their hearts, and who love the banner of Unculpsalm, and have respect unto the rulers chosen according to the Great Covenant, even although the men be not to their liking, and who are foolishly bent on destroying the armies and the power of them who would destroy the nation.

10. Wherefore we will not be seen listening to the gos-

pel of peace. For it shall be better for us to cry out for war, and meanwhile to hinder the war in secret, and to seek every occasion to bring the rulers of our country to scorn and derision in the time of her trial, and to aid Jeph the Repudiator, and his spies, and his emissaries, and to work confusion in the land.

11. For so shall the people be weary of their rulers, and bewildered with our confusion; and they shall trust us, and turn unto us in their desolation, and say, Verily, these are the men, and make us rulers of the land.

12. Then will we compromise ourselves again unto our masters the Tshivulree and the Phiretahs, as it is meet, and right, and pleasant for us to do; and we shall find yet deeper dust wherein to crawl before them; and we shall loosen the bonds of these provinces, and make each governor of a province thereof a little satrap, but great in his own eyes and in the eyes of the Phlunkees, which will surround him, that he may defy the chief ruler of the land; and we shall divide the spoil.

13. But these men came to the hall of Peter the Barrel-maker to hear Phernandiwud declare the new gospel of peace,

14. Din Ninny, who was chief ruler of the assembly, and who directed all the doings thereof; Isaiah, who was captain of the Hammerites; and many others of the sect of Smalphri among the Dimmichrats.

15. And with them there came a great multitude of the Hittites and the Hammerites, and of the Dedrabitz from Koubae beyond Boueree, and the dwellers in Phyvpintz, which is nigh unto the tombs where they buried Juz Tiss. (Now Juz Tiss was not of kin unto that Ker Tiss who wrote of the Great Covenant), and in Makkurilvil, and in the country as thou goest by the shore of the river on the East, unto Shyppyardz.

16. And all these men gathered themselves together, fiercely bent upon peace. And they filled the hall of Peter the Barrel-maker, and the open space round about.

17. And when Phernandiwud stood up and beckoned unto them they shouted for about the space of half an hour. For they remembered what he had done for them aforetime; and they looked for a ministration of the gospel of peace, such as there had been between the watchmen of Phernandiwud and those which had been appointed by the governor and rulers of the province. And they said within themselves, Now shall we again break the heads of the watchmen of Ken Edee; and there shall be peace again in the land.

18. And Phernandiwud said unto them, Hearken, O men of Gotham! I come before you this day preaching a new gospel of peace. Peace on earth and good-will to men. Peace on earth, that I and my faithful followers may get what is due unto us, and good-will unto men who are of our persuasion among the Dimmichrats.

19. For there be Dimmichrats, yea, verily, even Pahdees, who are not of our persuasion, and who enter not into our congregation. Let them be accursed.

20. And all the people said, Hi! hi! For such is the manner of the Hittites and the Hammerites of Gotham when they are well pleased.

21. And again Phernandiwud opened his mouth and said, O, my brethren, the day of calamity cometh upon the land of Unculpsalm, and there is no man able to help. Therefore have I come hither that I may save this nation. No man raiseth the banner of peace. Therefore will I raise it, that war and hate, which are the children of Satan, may be at an end, except for the Dimmichrats which are not of our persuasion, and the men of Belial which preach freedom unto the Niggah. Them let us hate with a perfect hatred, and upon them let us make war without ceasing.

22. (And when the Hittites and Hammerites heard of liberty to the Niggah, they all groaned with an exceeding loud groan, as it were if each man had been seized with

pangs of griping in his bowels. For to hear of freedom to the Niggah is gall and wormwood to the Hittites and the Hammerites.)

23. Then said Fernandiwud, Through the pride of their hearts, and the vanity and wickedness of their imaginations, the rulers of this land have sinned and done wickedly in that they have not allowed the Tshivulree and the Phiretahs to destroy this nation without making war upon it.

24. For the land of Unculpsalm hath no right to a government, neither have the people of Unculpsalm any right to be a nation. Neither is the Great Covenant a covenant to be kept, except by the men of each province, so long as it is pleasing in their eyes.

25. But these only are right, Peace and the everlasting Niggah. Such peace as we had aforetime, ere the accursed spirit Bak Bohn took possession of this people. Peace which will enable our brethren of the South to eat their bread in the sweat of another's face; to rob the laborer of his hire; to oppress the weak, and set their foot upon the neck of the lowly; to beat their Niggahs with many stripes, to hunt them with dogs, and to slay them; to take their women for concubines, and to beget of them sons and daughters; and to sell from the mother the fruit of her womb and the nursling of her bosom; to make merchandise of the fruit of their own loins, and to sell their own flesh and blood into bondage forever.

27. Peace, my brethren, which will also restore our right of free speech according to the Great Covenant; of which we have been robbed by the rulers of this land, that they may wage their wicked war upon the Phiretahs.

28. For, O men of Gotham, ye see this day how your rulers oppress you, and will allow no man to speak evil of them, that they may wage this war without let or hinderance; and that all men's mouths are shut by fear of the gallows or the dungeon, who will not prophesy smooth

things of their damnable doings, and cover up their wickedness and glorify their abominations.

29. Therefore I declare unto you that we must have the peace, the peace which ensueth from free speech. So that when men of Belial seek to turn the hearts of the men of the South to setting their bondsmen free, and taking away from us our everlasting Niggah, the Phiretahs may seize upon them, and beat them with many stripes, and hang them upon trees, and roast them with fire, and pour hot pitch upon them, and ride them upon sharp beams, very grievous to bestride. Peace and free speech, such as there was on the day when Prestenbruux smote down Charles the Summoner, and beat him until he was nigh unto death.

30. Let this Peace hover over the land, scattering balm from her outstretching wings. Balm for the wounded souls of the Tshivulree and the Phiretahs; balm for the wounds which Dimmichratic brethren have inflicted on each other; balm for my bruised spirit and defrauded expectations.

31. Let this peace come to us, my brethren, and the lion of the South and the lamb of the North shall lie down together, and there shall no more be contention between them; for the lamb shall be inside of the lion.

32. Let us then be lambs, O men of Gotham! Yea, let us be meek as lambs. For it is written that the meek shall inherit the earth.

32. Then the Hittites and the Hammerites again cried out Hi! hi! after their fashion; and in a twinkling many of them took an oath that they were the meek, and that they should inherit the earth.

34. Then Phernandiwud said, All now is well with us, my brethren, and with the land of Unculpsalm. Peace and free-speech shall prevail among us now and forever.

35. Then the Hittites and the Hammerites shouted with a great shout, and they clenched their fists and said, God

do so to us and more also, if we break not every man his head which saith there shall not henceforth be peace and free-speech throughout the land.

36. And no man answered. So they said, Lo there is peace.

37. And Phernandiwud said these things many times.

38. Now when Phernandiwudd had made an end of speaking unto the people, there arose Isaiah, he who was captain of a band of the Hammerites, and which was one of the chief disciples of Phernandiwud. And he said,

39. Shall there not be peace, my brethren? Remember ye not the time when Philip, the priest of Beelzebub came here preaching deliverance to the captive and the setting at liberty even of the Niggah? and how he entered into the Tabernacle and gathered unto him iniquitous men, men of Belial who hearkened unto him, and believed in him?

40. And remember ye not how I, with you Hammerites, who break the heads of all them who set themselves against you, and you, O Hittites, who hit from the shoulder, went into the Tabernacle and broke up their congregation and scattered their assembly?

41. And I knocked down Philip, and dragged him out of the pulpit wherein he was speaking, and drave him out of the Tabernacle?

42. Yea, verily, I knocked him down; for I am a man of peace; and dragged him out of his pulpit and drave him forth of the Tabernacle; for I love free speech.

43. Then the Hittites and the Hammerites and the Dimmichrats which had joined themselves unto the faction of Jeph the Repudiator, burst out into a great shouting. And for the space of about an hour they did nothing but cry Peace and Free Speech, and death unto him that sayeth to the contrary.

44. And when they were weary of shouting, they went each man unto his own home.

45. And the new gospel of peace spread abroad, and prevailed mightily.

46. And it went throughout all the land of Unculpsalm even beyond the border of Masunandicsun.

47. So that in about ten days the chief captain of the Tshivulree, whose name was Robbutleeh (he who had forced Litulmak, who was surnamed the Unready, to change his base, and sent Joseph, whose surname showeth that it was not he which fled from the wife of Potiphar, back from whence he came), took an army of the Phiretahs and marched into two of the provinces of the land of Unculpsalm, proclaiming the new gospel of peace at the point of the sword.

48. And he laid parts of those provinces waste with fire, and he destroyed the bridges that were over the rivers, and carried off their horses, and their corn and their cattle; and put all them that resisted the new gospel of peace to the sword.

49. So the people began to understand the mystery of the new gospel; and they glorified it; and they said, yet a little while, and the Niggah shall be restored to his bondage, and the Tshivulree, and the Phiretahs shall be our masters, and peace shall rule the land with a rod of iron, and we shall compromise ourselves for ever. And there was great rejoicing.

50. Now I, even I, Benjamin the scribe, the brother of Phernandiwud, have written these things, not of my own will, or of the promptings of my own heart, for the truth is not in me. But forasmuch as the spirit of prophecy hath descended upon me, like Balaam, the son of Beor, I have uttered the innermost thoughts of my heart in mine own despite, and I have written the mystery of the new gospel of peace.

51. And to few shall it be given to comprehend this mystery.

52. And the acts of Phernandiwud, whose walk was

slantindicular, and of his disciples, after the proclamation of the new gospel of peace, and of James the scribe, and of Erastus his brother, and of Samuel who is rich in butter, and Samuel who sendeth the lightning whither he will, and Hiram the publican, and that other Samuel, who ministered unto the Phiretah woman: and of Elijah, who smelleth the battle afar off in the tents of Tamunee; and of Cyrus, and Primus, and Kerr Tiss, and Isaiah of the Hammerites, which were Gentiles; and of Augustus, the money changer, which was of the circumcision, and of the other Pharisees and Phlunkees, shall not I, Benjamin the scribe, write them in a book? and they shall be spread abroad in all lands for the enlightening of all nations.